Words of a woman

Akhi Khan

Presentation by *BookLeaf Publishing*

Web: www.bookleafpub.com

E-mail: info@bookleafpub.com

ISBN: 9789357213806

First edition 2023

To Manna (Rohima): For showing me how to be a strong woman.

To Shahadat (Shadz): For being the best friend every niece needs.

To Jakir (Zak): For teaching me how to live in this world.

To Amma nana and Abba nana: For giving me such a rich childhood.

To Abir, Arif and Afreen: For being so caring everytime their sister fell ill.

To Mum (Shumi): For teaching me how to be a good person and supporting me through everything in life.

To Dad (Zia): For working such long shifts just so we can live an easily life.

To me (Akhi): You did it.

To All The Modern Day "Prophet Adams".

Dear 'Adam' of 2022,

Thank you dear Adam

for the donation

from your rib cage.

I appreciate it.

I really do.

But this donation,

does not mean

you have the right

to crush my ribs

when you realise

that I don't actually need your support and

I am fine without it.

- From 'Hawa,' 2022.

When he wants a taste of being a God.

Dear Husbands,

You can go on a pilgrimage -

ask God to wash away your sins,

bask in the holy light of your own righteousness.

But if I do the same,

I wonder why

the water does not wash off

the dark bruises on my body.

And if I stand in the light to see God

I just see shadows -

Why?

Because you stand in the way

and you refuse to be dethroned.

Abuse is a cancer

I used to love getting my hair cut as a child.

Amma would line my hair up,

all to a perfect length

and gently cut my tresses.

I cannot believe

I didn't realise

that being married to you

would mean free haircuts

every time you're mad

as the hair comes out in clumps

between your clenched fists.

When he finally decides to step up and cook.

Sometimes I feel like I am marinated meat.

Turmeric beneath my fingernails

coriander powder brushed over me

But only a pinch of masalas locked in my tresses
-

just because society doesn't like the women too fiery.

So, when I fell sick and said -

"I can't move my body to the kitchen".

You showed me your cooking skills -

and how passionate you were

To cook me.

Because it was your heavy body which crushed
into mine

your weight thrusted into mine

Your blood rushing -

Not mine.

I lay there flat.

A dead bird. cooked on the kitchen table.

You didn't need a stove.

The flames beneath your skin

Were strong enough -

Burning my body like rotten lamb on charcoal.

And that's how I finally realised,

You know how to cook.

But you only have the appetite

To cook me.

And I looked into your blazing eyes,

Fully aware that you were also ready

 to savour every bite of me.

When you kill your unborn daughters.

I can't lose the weight you want me to.

They're remnants of the dead children my womb has carried.

Little pieces of the little girls you killed,

All forming layers on me.

It's not fat.

It's their souls.

Their hearts.

Their unformed bodies.

All on me.

Awakening me.

Reviving me.

Igniting me.

I can't lose the weight you want me to .

I lost them once.

I can't lose them again.

The fem-artyr.

I have eras of stories.

About heroes, and their conquers all

laced and sewn into my existence.

I would not be stood here today,

If all the other warriors before me

did not fight for my livelihood.

Soldiers die for their countries,

We die for our future sisters.

I have other limbs too.

I was forced into silence.

My lips swiped off of my face from your gnarly
hands.

Funny.

You forgot one thing:

you can take away my voice -

stitch my lips with wired thread and

burn my mouth alive.

But you

Can't take away

the story which my hands

Are dying to write.

I have other limbs too.

Where did it all go wrong?

12

They say husbands are a wife's garment.

Garment?

Oh the irony.

Because you

you rip my garments off me

almost every single day

The way I'd love to rip

our tarnished nikkah documents.

Seasoned from assault.

13

I am young.

So I taste bland.

Not exactly seasoned with experience.

Plain, without the exotic spices you wanted.

So you decided to flavour me with

your acidic juice.

Squeezing it between my thighs,

and it stings as it slides down my legs.

I am still young.

But now I taste sour.

Seasoned with bitter experience.

One life for another.

They say a womb is like a home -

A mimicry of God,

the giver of life.

They say it can nourish a soul

into existence,

It has space for a whole life

To blossom.

Isn't that just beautiful?

So when God decided

That my body could not handle sustaining life,

I sat there counting all my sins on my fingers.

If I could ask for mercy,

For every single sin,

Maybe I'd be forgiven.

Every time I do a good deed,

I'll put a finger down.

One less sin.

One step closer to a child.

When I told you the news,

I took it as God making my job easier.

Maybe it was a sign that God had forgiven me.

Because when I told you,

you broke every single finger

with your hard fisted knuckles.

I know I can't give life.

I apologise.

Do you want me to compensate?

You can take mine in exchange.

When forever doesn't end.

Isn't it weird?

Life is something so transient,

And we live a fleeting existence.

To be bound forever to someone,

Is a lie.

All lies.

No-one is going to be there,

When you're buried 6 feet underground.

For some people,

That thought saddens them.

The idea that one day they have to depart from their better half,

And lie there alone in their graves.

For me,

It brings joy and comfort.

I cannot wait

To escape your claws.

For women to bathe me before I am put to rest,

See the deep bruises you have imprinted on me

And pick out your fingernails from my skin.

For me,

Death is my escape.

And whilst this life is transient,

It feels like it's lasting forever whilst I'm with
you.

Craving Company

My soul is bleeding away.

And the cage surrounding it

Is just broken bones.

It's

Weak,

Feeble,

Malnourished.

It aches to exist.

She's no longer weeping for strength,

She just wants a bandage.

Just a small one to stop the bleeding.

And then you came in.

You swooped right in

Like the angel you are

and stitched it up.

You used your golden thread of joy,

To sew it back to life.

You want it to heal.

You want it to be okay.

I know you do.

But I fear it's too late.

I'm beyond healing.

Because when you come in everyday to tend to
my bruised soul,

The demons in my mind come out at night

And unravel your doings.

But, I don't mind.

I don't mind not being able to heal.

I just want you here, with me.

Tend to my aching soul everyday,

Even though I know I can't get through this.

Because I just crave your presence,

As I bleed away slowly.

I may not have had peace whilst I was alive,

But I can have peace when I die if you're beside me.

The Princess And Prince cHARMing

Fairy tales aren't real.

It's the one basic rule that's drilled into the adult mind.

Don't hope. Don't hope. Don't hope.

And yet my heart will be defiant.

It just will not listen.

I will imagine the most beautiful dreams every time I close my eyes.

I yearn for the most precious moments every time a tear rolls down my cheek.

I escaped reality so much that when I was catapulted back into it, I convinced myself that I was magical.

I am capable of making fairy tales into a reality. It's just my fault my life is not all picture perfect.

So I try these tricks, these spells, these prayers,

To make you into a good man.

I want to love you with every fibre of my body
and every inch of my soul.

I really do.

But you turn my fairy tales into poison, every
time you coil your hands around my neck like a
snake.

I make this same stupid mistake every time:

Fairy tales can exist.

Just not with you, because you're just a beast
impersonating a man.

And I don't have the magic to turn you into
Prince Charming.

Don't hope.

Don't hope.

Don't hope.

One Last Time

You wake up in the morning, and force yourself
to draw the curtains.

You're not ready to face another day of living, of
existing, of hurting.

The sun is shining bright, and you cup all the
sunlight you can manage.

It feels so precious, to just feel it in your palms.

Besides, you need all the light you can get to
resuscitate your near-dead soul.

Then, he comes from behind.

Maybe he's going to open his hands,

Feel the sweet rays of light between his
fingertips too.

Instead, he opens his palms out,

And an engulfing darkness emerges out of them.

Impaling the light in your hands.

He cages you in this dark, like a flightless bird
with nowhere to go.

Now you're too scared to leave, because this
darkness is all you've ever known.

And yet, your heart craves to taste the light, just
one last time

before you go.

Stars are our sisters

25

When I was younger, I was told the stars above
are our dead mothers.

So from a young age, I have always felt
connected to the galaxy above,

The breath-taking artistry etched into the sky.

Especially the stars,

randomly splurged across the navy canvas.

Everyone loves their beauty.

But does anyone ever stop to think

How cold they must feel?

How uncomfortable they must feel -

Mercilessly stretched above us,

Just for us to eye and ogle at?

Our dead mothers, who died whilst reclaiming
the womanhood pumping in their veins.

It's so sad.

Because even after their death, they're just made
to cruelly shine bright,

When all they want to do is just quietly live.

Didn't they get enough of that when they were
alive?

A new start.

You are above me and I am beneath you.

You have the power to swallow me whole,

And then spit me out when you don't like the taste.

You could snap my neck like a twig, and force your weight on me like a paralytic induced dream.

What do you do instead?

You give me your soft hand,

So I can take it and crawl up from the dark,

To sit there beside you in the light.

I sit in the palace you have created for us,

In awe of how you have made enough room

For the pain I carry.

Suddenly, I realise,

Is this what love is?

You've used your own precious hands,

To build a stage

Just for me.

The spotlight is shining bright

And it's just on me.

You let me say my story,

And don't interrupt me once,

Because this stage -

It's just for me.

On the days where I don't want to be fierce

Because the world is too cruel an audience,

I feel safe enough to crawl into your open arms

And bury my face into your chest -

The perfect hiding place.

You are my new start.

My new story,

And I am terrified of what's going to be written
in the next pages.

So you've given me the pen.

You quietly sit there behind me,

Backstage,

Wiping my tears as I write,

so it doesn't smudge the ink.

I wait for you to give up on me.

To feel the erupting anger,

And rip out the pages of this story.

It happens every time.

I'm waiting for you to follow your ancestors.

I watch you,

As you read each page.

I hold my breath,

My jaw eagerly waiting for the fist.

But instead you press your thumb against it

And look over me with that gorgeous grin.

It's not anger I see in you.

It's pride.

Suddenly I realised.

This is what love is.

That feeling you get in that exact moment.

To be

Perhaps there will be a day in the near future,
when you will be too feeble to hold my hand and
too weary to kiss me. Perhaps there will be a day
in the future, when I will be laying on your chest
but my ears are too weak to hear the music of
your beating heart. Perhaps there will be a day,
where we are too frail to wrap our arms around
each other for comfort when the world is being
cruel.

But I will still be there, because your presence is
enough. It's enough to pump my veins with
sweet, beautiful colours. It's enough to make me
feel alive, even if my body is collapsing
inwardly. Your presence, even if it is weak,
even if it is silent, feeble, frail. It is enough. It
will always be enough.

I just need you to be. That's all I ask for. Please.
Just be.

From, us.

My mind was undressed in front of him. He's been through the architecture, scoured every corner for every silly, immature joke in there. I laugh with joy, because I'm happy. I don't mind him seeing it at all, to see all of me.

But then, he discovers a box, bolted and locked. I'd forgotten about that.

I swear it was sealed shut, but he pries it open. And with that, everything is unleashed again. The pain. The demons. The tears. I tremble in fear, as the wounds reopen. Maybe he'll skin me alive, because the scars are too ugly for him to handle. Maybe he'll burn them with acid, so the skin is shiny and new for him to taint. I wait for him, ready to endure whichever decision he takes.

Instead, he stares at them, poking and prodding. He comes close, caresses each one, leaves soft fluttering kisses on every wound like tiny butterflies. I could see his gleaming eyes, whispering quiet I-love-yous. Yet, I could feel his heart shrieking it:

"I do not love you in parts. I love you, whole
and complete, broken and shattered."

I weep.

He's made enough space for the both of us in his
heart. For me, the girl that exists right now in
this moment as she speaks to you. But also who
I was, the girl with baggage tied to her weak
body, broken bones and broken dreams.

So this is a thank you, (from the both of us).

www.ingramcontent.com/pod-product-compliance
Lightning Source LLC
Chambersburg PA
CBHW050751180726

48003CB00020B/2335